AT THE STARTING LINE

MOTORSPORTS

Kaitlyn Duling

Rourke

ROURKE'S
SCHOOL to HOME
CONNECTIONS

BEFORE AND DURING READING ACTIVITIES

Before Reading: *Building Background Knowledge and Vocabulary*

Building background knowledge can help children process new information and build upon what they already know. Before reading a book, it is important to tap into what children already know about the topic. This will help them develop their vocabulary and increase their reading comprehension.

Questions and Activities to Build Background Knowledge:

1. Look at the front cover of the book and read the title. What do you think this book will be about?
2. What do you already know about this topic?
3. Take a book walk and skim the pages. Look at the table of contents, photographs, captions, and bold words. Did these text features give you any information or predictions about what you will read in this book?

Vocabulary: *Vocabulary Is Key to Reading Comprehension*

Use the following directions to prompt a conversation about each word.

- Read the vocabulary words.
- What comes to mind when you see each word?
- What do you think each word means?

Vocabulary Words:

- *demolition derby*
- *drag race*
- *drone*
- *motorsports*
- *pylons*
- *race circuits*

During Reading: *Reading for Meaning and Understanding*

To achieve deep comprehension of a book, children are encouraged to use close reading strategies. During reading, it is important to have children stop and make connections. These connections result in deeper analysis and understanding of a book.

Close Reading a Text

During reading, have children stop and talk about the following:

- Any confusing parts
- Any unknown words
- Text to text, text to self, text to world connections
- The main idea in each chapter or heading

These strategies will help children learn to analyze the text more thoroughly as they read.

When you are finished reading this book, turn to the next-to-last page for **After-Reading Questions** and an **Activity**.

TABLE OF CONTENTS

Start Your Engines 4
Around the Track 6
Off-Road Warriors 12
Sky and Sea 18
A Need for Speed 24
Memory Game 30
Index 31
After-Reading Questions 31
Activity 31
About the Author 32

START YOUR ENGINES

If you have a need for speed, hop in the driver's seat! In **motorsports**, there are countless races to be run—and won.

motorsports (MOH-tur-sportz): competitions between motorized vehicles

The first motorsport race took place in 1894. Cars drove 50 miles (80 kilometers) from Paris to Rouen, France. Their average speed was just 10.2 miles per hour (mph) (16.4 kilometers per hour (kmh))!

Are you ready to watch today's cars, trucks, motorcycles, and other vehicles as they compete to cross the finish line?

3...2...1...let's go!

AROUND THE TRACK

Early competitions had cars racing from city to city. Over the years, enclosed tracks or **race circuits** became popular. Organizers could invite paying customers to watch the action!

The Indianapolis Motor Speedway in Speedway, Indiana, is known as the Racing Capital of the World.

The Indianapolis Motor Speedway

race circuits (RASE sir-cuts): courses over which races are run

Some circuits are flat ovals. Others are curvy and hilly. The Nürburgring Nordschleife race track in Germany is one of them. It has 154 corners!

Nürburgring Nordschleife

Different race circuits host different types of races. Car races usually feature one of two types: open-wheel or closed-wheel.

The wheels on open-wheel cars are outside the car's body. Formula and IndyCar are two famous types of open-wheel racing. The cars are expensive. They are some of the fastest in the world.

open-wheel car

The wheels on closed-wheel cars are under the car's body. NASCAR is the most popular form of closed-wheel racing in the United States.

PIT STOP

During a race, drivers make pit stops. In the pit, a team can add fuel to the car, change the tires, and make repairs. They work safely and quickly. They get the car ready to reenter the race.

Some races last for hours. Others take just a few seconds! A **drag race** uses a special, straight course called a dragstrip. In a drag race, cars race to see which one can speed up the fastest. Whoever crosses the finish line first, wins!

drag race (drag rase): a competition in which drivers race side by side on a flat, straight course

Have you ever tried go-kart racing? Indoor and outdoor circuits can be found across the globe. It's fun to race with friends.

There are professional go-kart races too! The pros get paid to race. Their custom karts can speed faster than 100 mph (161 kmh)!

OFF-ROAD WARRIORS

Off-road races are held anywhere but the road. Some drive on dirt. Others cruise through the desert or zoom across the beach. They can plow through mud and over mountains.

Ice racing is the coolest off-road race of them all, literally! Most ice racers ride motorcycles.

THE ELECTRIC ODYSSEY

Extreme E is an off-road race that started in 2021. Electric SUVs compete in remote parts of the world. Organizers want the race to make people aware of the changing climate.

Motorcycle racers must be brave. They can't hide from the weather or the dirt. One popular form of motorcycle racing is motocross. These motorcycles are sometimes called dirt bikes.

MOTORCYCLE MADNESS

The Baja 1000 is known as North America's "most dangerous race." Motorcycles race hundreds of miles through Mexico's desert. It gets hot and messy!

Motocross races are held on off-road circuits. There are lots of hills and plenty of mud. Sometimes four-wheel vehicles called ATVs or quads compete too.

Crash! Thud. Eeek! This doesn't sound like a race. That's because it's not a race at all. It's a **demolition derby**. These cars are crashing into each other on purpose. In a demo derby, the last car that can still drive is the winner.

Demo derbies are often held in muddy fields. The mud helps to slow down the cars. This can make it safer. All glass is removed from the cars and drivers wear safety gear.

demolition derby (dem-uh-LISH-uhn DUR-bee): events in which vehicles slam into each other

If you really want to crush a car, you can use a monster truck. These off-road trucks are huge! They are often around 12 feet (3.7 meters) tall. Monster trucks race, jump, and flip.

SKY AND SEA

Some race around a circuit. Others go off-road. But what about a race across the sky? Motorsport races can happen almost anywhere!

The first powered airplane launched in 1903. Just a few years later, in 1909, the world's first air race was held. Pilots have been battling it out ever since.

Some air races are over in minutes. Some take days! In the Air Race Classic, teams of women pilots compete to fly across the United States.

The Reno Air Races is one of the biggest air racing events in the world. In Reno, Nevada, pilots race around a course marked by tall **pylons**. They fly around the outside of the pylons. Some racing jets fly up to 500 mph (805 kmh)!

pylons (PYE-lahns): tall, brightly colored poles marking an air-race course

Airplanes compete in drag races too. The winner is the plane that lands at the finish line first.

Boat racing dates back to ancient China. Today, powerboats zip across the water at super-high speeds! They have a skinny, pointed shape. This helps them cut through the water.

Long, narrow boats called dragon boats were raced in ancient China, and still are today!

Offshore races take place in the ocean. Inshore races happen on lakes and rivers. There, boats make quick turns around buoys. All powerboat races have one thing in common: extremely fast boats!

SWAMP BUGGY RACING

Naples, Florida, is home to a special race. Swamp buggies have huge wheels. They are part car, part boat! They race through muddy marshes and swamps.

A NEED FOR SPEED

Watching professional racing is fun. But you don't have to be a pro to line up at the starting line! You don't even need a driver's license. There are many forms of youth racing.

Kids as young as three can drive go-karts. Quarter midgets are small cars that can race on dirt or concrete. Bandolero cars look like miniature NASCAR cars! There are even junior drag races.

quarter midget

go-kart

dragster

What if you could race from your living room? Simulation racing looks and feels like real racing. It's just missing the car. Simulators move and make sounds as though you're really on the track.

drone (drohn): an aircraft that is controlled remotely

Drone racing is becoming more and more popular. Pilots stay safe on the ground while flying drones through a set course. Sometimes there are obstacles. Each drone has a video camera. The drone pilot wears a camera too

Some drivers want to race while finishing their chores. So they race lawn mowers! Actually, the blades are removed, but the mowers still have engines. Instead of grass lawns, they drive on dirt tracks. Those are some serious mowers!

Are you ready to race? Start your engine! With so many different types of motorsports, there's something for every racer. All it takes is a little bravery ... and a whole lot of speed.

MEMORY GAME

Look at the pictures. What do you remember reading on the pages where each image appeared?

INDEX

airplane(s) 18, 21
boat(s) 22, 23
car(s) 5, 6, 8, 9, 10, 16, 17, 23, 24, 26
go-kart(s) 11, 24, 25
monster truck(s) 17
motocross 14, 15
motorcycle(s) 5, 13, 14, 15
off-road 12, 13, 15, 17, 18

AFTER-READING QUESTIONS

1. Why do you think people enjoy motorsports?
2. What are three different types of motorsport?
3. How are open-wheel and closed-wheel racing different?
4. Why would a race car or motorcycle racer need to be brave?
5. What are some ways in which you could get involved in motorsports?

ACTIVITY

New and interesting vehicles keep motorsports exciting. It's your turn to design the racing vehicle of your dreams! Draw your own race car, motorcycle, or go-kart. Give your dream vehicle a name. Write a short description of where it races, how fast it goes, and what it's like to drive it.

ABOUT THE AUTHOR

Kaitlyn Duling may not own a race car ... but she does love to drive. She remembers watching NASCAR with her grandad. When she's not in the driver's seat, Kaitlyn is writing in Boston, Massachusetts. She has authored over 100 books for kids and teens, including many about race cars!

www.rourkebooks.com

PHOTO CREDITS:
cover, title page: ©action sports/ Shutterstock.com, ©Rainer Herhaus/ Shutterstock.com, ©Anastasija Popova/ Shutterstock.com, ©Lyle Setter/ Icon Sportswire DHT/Lyle Setter/Icon Sportswire/Newscom; pages 4-7, 12-13, 18-19, 24-25: ©Yngvarr/ Shutterstock.com; pages 4-5: ©action sports/ Shutterstock.com; page 5: ©National Motor Museum / Heritage Images/Newscom; page 6, 30: ©ciapix/ Shutterstock.com; page 7: ©Florent Gooden/ Dppi/ZUMAPRESS/Newscom, ©Florent Gooden/Dppi/ZUMAPRESS/Newscom; page 8: ©lev radin/ Shutterstock.com; page 9: ©Fabio Pagani/ Shutterstock.com, ©Bruce Alan Bennett/ Shutterstock.com; page 10: ©Dannie Walls / Icon SMI CBB/Dannie Walls / Icon SMI/Newscom, ©Grindstone Media Group/ Shutterstock.com; page 11: ©Robert Hardholt/ Shutterstock.com, ©977_ReX_977/ Shutterstock.com; page 12, 30: ©Rodrigo Garrido/ Shutterstock.com; page 12: ©Eric Gevaert/ Shutterstock.com, ©Nachaliti/ Shutterstock.com; page 13: ©Sergei Kaliganov/ Shutterstock.com, ©Volodymyr Dvornyk/ Shutterstock.com; page 14: ©vm/ Getty Images, ©Alan_Lagadu/ Getty Images; page 15: ©Stan Sholik/ZUMA Press/Newscom, ©Pukhov K/ Shutterstock.com; page 16: ©Aaron of L.A. Photography/ Shutterstock.com; page 17, 30: ©Grindstone Media Group/ Shutterstock.com; page 18, 30: ©Historica Graphica Collection / Heritage Images/Newscom, page 18: ©akg-images/Newscom; page 19: ©Ania Freindorf/SIPA/Newscom, ©Ania Freindorf/SIPA/Newscom; pages 20-21: ©Jeff Schultes/ Shutterstock.com, ©CHEN WS/ Shutterstock.com; page 22, 30: ©windmoon/ Shutterstock.com; page 22: ©DPST/Newscom; page 23: ©Steven Paston/ZUMA Press/Newscom, ©Art Seitz/ABACAUSA.COM/ Newscom; page 24: ©Image Craft/ Shutterstock.com, ©Gunter Nezhoda/ Shutterstock.com; page 25: ©David Allio/Icon SMI 951/David Allio/Icon SMI/ Newscom, ©Jonathan Wong/SCMP/Newscom, ©Michael Allio/Icon Sportswire 116/Michael Allio/Icon Sportswire/Newscom; page 26: ©Aisyaqilumaranas/ Shutterstock.com; page 27, 30: ©Yanosh Nemesh/ Shutterstock.com; page 27: ©Kietisak Yaemklebbua/ Shutterstock.com; page 28: ©Felix K stle/dpa/ picture-alliance/Newscom; page 29: ©andresr/ Getty Images

Edited by: Laura Malay
Cover design by: Alison Tracey
Interior design by: Alison Tracey

Library of Congress PCN Data

Motorsports / Kaitlyn Duling
(At the Starting Line)
ISBN 978-1-73165-733-6 (hardcover)
ISBN 978-1-73165-720-6 (softcover)
ISBN 978-1-73165-746-6 (e-book)
ISBN 978-1-73165-759-6 (e-pub)
Library of Congress Control Number: 2023933033

Rourke Educational Media
Printed in the United States of America
03-2162511937